I0086949

The

Life

We

Live

Other books written by Justin Z. Stingley... **Love & Life the Poetic Book**...

The Life We Live

A Poetic Book

By

Justin Z. Stingley

Editors

Shelly Flowers
Sharene Terry
Angela Thomas
Jessica Norman
Justin Stingley

Cover Designers

Latasha Stingley
Justin Stingley

Copyright © 2010, 2011 by Justin Z. Stingley
All rights reserved.

ISBN: 978-0-578-08234-9

Published by: Justin Z. Stingley
Park Forest, IL.
USA

To learn more about the author/publisher contact him via email: justinzstingley@sbcglobal.net

To learn more about his publications visit: www.lulu.com/spotlight/stingley

*Special thank you to Deidre Glover, Yalonda Mason & Shelly Flowers with the editing of my first book: **<u>Love & Life the Poetic Book</u>** and to my Parents, Family, & Friends for your loving support.*

With Love & Thanks,

Justin Z. Stingley

The Life We Live

From the life I live
To the life we live,

I share with you
All that I can give,

The drama, the tears
Not knowing where to turn,

The past mistakes
From which we have learned,

The liking of someone
Without providing a name,

To walking through life
Confused and ashamed,

And still
Questions remain,

Do we all
Feel the same,

Think the same
Carry the same weight,

Instead of talking
Do we always debate,

Maybe argue or fight
Just to past the time,

Ready to quit
At the drop of a dime,

Because encouragement for us
Is hard to find,

And gloomy days
Cover over the sun shine,

To Whom It May Concern
Here's a thought for you,

Ask yourself
Do I live my life true,

True to myself
And others around me,

Or do I hide the truth
So that they won't see,

Do I look for the light
To shine upon my day,

And try to look at things
In a positive way,

No matter what the days bring
No matter what they may give,

Always be true
In the life that you live...

Thank You and Enjoy,

Justin Z. Stingley

Contents

A

Life

Lived

A Life Lived

So many lost but not forgotten,
Like a good plant when spoiled or rotten,

The memories we have to help us get by,
Sad to say it's still hard to cry,

For others it's not, truth be told,
They take it back, but you're so cold,

I regret not reading the letters you sent,
I wish I told you how much you meant,

The laughs, the conversation,
The jokes and humiliation,

The meals you prepared
And how you brought us together,

Back then
No one cared about the weather,

The time together was worth more than gold,
As we enjoyed every moment, never to be sold,

But to be remembered, your name, your style
You, who is missed so much,

As you continue to change
The lives you touched,

A life lived
A life worth living,

Is a life
That still keeps on giving……

Anonymous

The morning star gets brighter as a smile's upon your face,

I only ask if I could take its place,

So that I to can shine as bright as the sun,

With a smile like that life must be fun,

It seems though a cloud will sit upon this day,

Because I can not get you to even look my way,

Oh how I would love for you to know my name,

But it seems to me, you may not feel the same,

Knowing this can been the first time we could have met,

I hide myself and this I will regret,

With smiles all around and not a frown to be found,

I hope this letter does not hit the ground....

I Want to Know

I may not know you but yet I want to stay,
I do not want us to go our separate way,

You may not know me but I yearn for you,
I love all of the things you do,

I may not know you but I'm willing to learn,
Your trust and love is what I must earn,

You may not know me, but I give you my heart,
I extend my love to you though we are far apart,

I may not know you, but I do in a way,
You know I don't want to leave so I choose to stay,

Yet you don't know me, so with that I will leave,
But yet if I do will your heart start to grieve,

We may not know each other yet in a way we do,
By the love you have for me and mine for you.....

A Special Night

Now after all that was read and typed out today,

The question remains will it happen one day,

Will I be strolling through your block during the midnight hour,

Standing at your door holding a flower,

Gazing into your eyes yearning for your touch,

The smile on your face shows me you want me as much,

I reach for your hand and you reach for mine,

Before I speak you finish my line,

Our thoughts lead to something we both want and need,

You hand me a paper I say, "but," you say "shh just read,"

The note say "y for yes n for no,"

My heart beats fast as I say "yes let's go,"

So to the room we go as I place you on the bed,

I reach for the pillow so you can relax your head,

Turn off the light no need for that now,

I ask do you want it, you say "give it to me," I say "how,"

You say on top, I said "wow I'm surprised,"

"Why" you asked, as I say "I didn't know you like cheese on your fries,"

As we sit back and watch some TV,

Where did you think I was going this poem is PG...

The Affects of Life

How can I love you
With no reason at all,

Why should I talk to you
With no reason to call,

The choices I make now
Will affect my life ahead,

Why did I sleep with you
In my parents bed,

Why was I not thinking
Why did I not say stop,

It felt wrong at first
Until I got on top,

It should not have happened
It should not have taken place,

But yet it did happen
Why did I not play it safe,

The choices I make now
Will affect my life ahead,

I wish I would have listened
To what my mother said,

You always love your first
It's a special bond you share,

But when ours was over
You acted like you didn't care,

For me, or
For what we have done,

As I struggle each day
Bearing our son,

Time has gone
And so have you,

As a young mother
What am I to do,

The decisions we made then
Affect the life we live today,

Don't follow in your parent's footsteps son
Your mother would want it this way……

If You

If you seen the things that I've seen,

Would you choose to be blind,

If you knew the things that I know,

Would you be able to sleep at night,

If you live the life that I live,

Could you have survived,

If you walk the road that I walked,

Would you be ready to be judged,

If you smell the way that I smell,

Would you wash away the shame,

If you look the way that I look,

Should I turn the other way when you walk by,

If you are as educated as I am and life is good,

Then why is life so hard for you until you see me…

Not to Be Lost

At the end of this, my time might be up,
As I write you I drink from my cup,

From day one I was on my own,
No one to talk to, I'm all alone,

Until the day I came across Mr. Cool,
He had no laws he had no rules,

Just conversation was his word,
And he let me sleep just like a bird,

Until the day the crew got upset,
Said I was loud and I needed to jet,

Mr. Cool said, "Everything will be ok,"
The crew said "today is his last day,"

Time had past and days went by,
Every day I thought I would die,

But the next day what do I see,
Encouragement was waiting for me,

Surprised I was, and happy as well,
Until the day everything just fell,

The show must go on, no time to stop,
Even though this fellow host decided to drop,

Alone, no coolness, or encouragement at all,
Now I fear I might drop the ball,

With the way things are I know I might lose,
I fight every day and I try to refuse,

I look for help but there's no rescue for me,
I pray every day I'm down on one knee,

I try to turn to those that I feel can assist,
But they come and go like morning mist,

They may sprinkle me a little but not enough,
Every day is hard every day is rough,

Survival I look forward to if I can,
Wondering why no one will lend me a hand,

Did I do any wrong did I do any harm,
Did I cause panic did I cause an alarm,

Sources I seek to help me through such times,
Just leave me be to write my rhymes,

So as I start write I begin to seek,
I write so as not to become weak,

I show love to everyone that is in need,
Please, I beg you don't let me be a lost seed...

My Style

Is my style to boring too old fashioned,

What happened to showing love & compassion,

Feeling warmth for the words that you intake,

Putting you at ease like a smooth mellow lake,

Feeling the emotions of the writer and what they went through,

Maybe you might be experiencing such things too,

We all need relief, a time to get away,

And what wonders such words would do today,

So before you dismiss this style of writing that you feel is old,

Think of it as gold and the value it holds,

Let the words show its worth to you,

Before you dismiss my writings too…

The Day I Cry

The days I cry have special meaning to me,

Like the day I fell off an apple tree,

Also the day when I fell off my bike,

And when a girl told me to take a hike,

 Also when I got a whooping that really hurts too,

Especially over the things I know I didn't do,

But today I cry for a different reason in life,

Like the day when I married my wife,

Or the day I found some true friends,

With strong bonds that are hard to bend,

And even when times seem rough and tough,

The love they give is just enough,

But still from time to time I might sit back and cry,

And I look to God, to answer me why,

But soon all these tears that we see will be wiped away,

Because God had promised that it will happen one day…

How Deep are Your Roots

Where were you born
From whose tree did you fall,

Are the roots still strong
Does the tree stand tall,

From past years to now
Do you know if it has grown,

Have you written a letter; left a message
Via E-mail or cell phone,

Do you know if branches
Extend from your tree,

If so how many are there
Have you even cheeked to see,

How strong is the bond
That keeps the tree together,

Do you think it can survive
The most severe weather,

And of what health
Is your tree cared for,

When it is weak
Do you open your door,

To nurture it, strengthen it
To help it grow strong and tall,

Or do you sit back and watch
Its branches will fall,

Do you extend your hand
To help the tree rise,

Or do you sit back and watch
As your tree cries,

Regardless of how you may feel
About the branches on the tree,

You should never neglect, but respect
Your family history......

My Life

To the ones that don't know me, listen real good,
To the life I lived that only few understood,

Growing up it always seemed weird,
Scared over things that I never feared,

Sounds of laughter and the doing of right,
Never did I want to go to sleep at night,

My first girl was special to me,
Everything was good as far as I could see,

She was cool at first but then things went wrong,
Her girls started putting their noses where it didn't belong,

Asking what has he done for you, where do you go,
What do you do, who do you know,

So it was over for us and time for a new start,
Where I found my true love, the love of my heart,

As time developed so did we,
Can you believe I got down on one knee,

And a new start got even better with a little spice,
No longer was I eating just beans and rice,

Everything seemed so good and so great,
But I won't say there was never a complaint,

All couples have their ups and downs,
And some smiles turn into frowns,

But it's those that choose to work it out,
That helps others appreciate what love is about,

Now I can continue on for days about my life,
The house, the kid and the wife,

But to sum up my life, I share this with you,
The best recipe is to have a life too,

Theirs more to life than what you see,
Even though you may not believe me...

My First Love & Look at Life

From all walks of life, we come and we go,

For some of us, it's hard to say no,

The things we may go through and the things we face,

Sometime those things may put a smile on our face,

From every day Life we have come to learn,

With the Love in our hearts we have come to earn,

Knowledge, Truth, Respect, the doing of Right,

While spending time with those who we love at night,

This is not my first and it will not be my last,

Even as time seem to be moving fast,

As I wrote the first word I stopped to take a look,

Next I turned around and see a completed book,

A story to be told I share with you,

What once was one now became two......

The

Journal

The Journal

From every day to every hour,

As sugar is to sweet and salt is to sour,

From the best to the worst,

And from praise to cursed,

We take note of the things we do,

Our joys and our sorrows too,

We write them down and still move ahead,

But never forgetting what was said,

Or done as we turn back to look,

Into The Journal our most precious book…

A Good Day for Me

Within a week a lot has happened
Parties, parties and gift wrapping,

But today there's a certain vibe in the air
The weather was nice mostly fair,

Through the week, questions were running through my head
Should I get up or stay in the bed,

But today without hesitation I'm up and about
Ready to start my day and move on out,

Strange as it may seem I was ready for work
And I didn't care if so-n-so acted like a jerk,

I did what was needed to be done
After work I was on the run,

But before I left I said bye to my boss
I'm thinking did they put something in my sauce,

And as I start to turn the knob
I was asked to stay late on my job,

Still cheerful I had to refuse
But I'll come in early to be used,

Instead of running I walked to my train
To my surprise there was no rain,

Weatherman lied and my train is on time
And guess what I found a dime,

On such a beautiful day like today
Who cares what happens in May,

For now I'm happy nothing bad to report,
The next day may have problems for me to sort,

Or maybe tomorrow won't be so bad
So far in the journal I wrote nothing sad...

Waiting to Get Off

If you can only understand the pain that I feel,

Work was hard you know the deal,

Co-workers being lazy, all they do is talk,

They need to lose weight, jog, maybe walk,

Talking on the phone at least 80 times a day,

Then my manager has the nerve to ask me to stay,

I'm doing half her work already,

And why is dude asking me to call him when ready,

This isn't high school, I go to clubs,

I don't ride buses, I ride on dubs,

So when I leave this nightmare, the one they call job,

I might hang out with Bill, Crystal or Bob,

Better yet I might go home and relax my feet,

While listening to smooth and mellow beats,

As I run a hot bath with a little champagne,

To ease my stress and my pain,

Being at ease no worries at all,

Unplug the phone, don't want any calls,

But for now, I have 2 more hours to go,

Perfection is for this evening and tomorrow you'll know....

School is Crazy

Can you believe what happened in class,

She tried to cut dude with a piece of glass,

Teacher broke it up and security came,

Everybody cheering on like it was a game,

School isn't the same since the 8th grade,

It seems to have turned a darker shade,

But for now I'll strive to pass,

Dear journal I really can't stand this class…

My Greedy Man

I can't believe how selfish he is,
He won't even help me with our kids,

All I ask is to "feed them," that's all,
Instead he leaves to go play ball,

On Sunday I ask if he can dress them for me,
He says "its Sunday just leave them be",

I never known someone to be so cold,
The truth will hurt every time it is told,

Then he has the audacity to ask me for sex,
I told him you better go ask DEX,

Do you see how tired I am,
I have been working all day from A.M. to P.M.

He has the nerve to treat me like a slave,
Last I check we don't live in a cave,

Taking care of these kids and this house is my life,
A task I love once I became his wife,

Yet, he don't treat me the way I want to feel,
He lies so much I don't know fake from real,

He don't help me with the kids or around this house,
To think this is the man I made my spouse,

But that's okay I always say,
I need to live for the next day,

I can't get worked up over this wannabe man,
I'll go relax and lay under the fan,

And I'll leave you journal with these few words
My husband is equivalent to two fat turds…

The Worse Day for Me

O' my God what a day,

It was so bad I don't know what to say,

Blood pressure went up, sugar is low,

I'm about 20 minutes from falling to the floor,

Too many questions, too many concerns,

Pay me more money and increase my earns,

It makes no sense how these people act,

They act like they were born with no tact,

Respect me and I'll respect you,

Start something and I will start something too,

I can't wait till this week is over,

Maybe tomorrow things will be slower,

Better yet I'll just stay home and in the bed,

Next time journal with no more to be said…

My Nagging Woman

Here we go again and again,

Does she want an award or hand,

I took out the trash what have you done,

Keep on talking I might buy a gun,

All she does is what a woman should do,

Cook clean and wash the clothes too,

And play the role for her man in bed,

I didn't stutter you heard what I said,

That's when she really gets her reward,

But for now journal I am bored,

And when she finishes up with her last word,

I'll say, "Ok Hun" and "yes I heard…"

Cold Weather

Today things couldn't get any better,

No hat no glove no jacket no sweater,

I thought it was going to be nice today,

Boy was I wrong as I turned the other way,

Going around the corner it got even colder,

Bones ache so bad I feel I'm getting older,

Wrapped my arms together just to stay warm,

Chicago weather is in rare form,

As I think of a place where I can get heat,

Take my clothes off and warm my feet,

But for now I have to keep walking in the cold,

So till next time journal, I'm putting you on hold…

To

Whom

It

May

Concern

To Whom It May Concern

With all that we go through and all that we face,

Do you feel that you have a lot to waste,

Your time, your money, better yet your life,

In the dealings of everyday pains and strife,

Or maybe headaches and frustration as the list goes on,

Things you wish for just to be gone,

But how do you address such issues and help others to learn,

By writing it down addressed To Whom It May Concern......

What is He Up To

To whom it may concern
I would like to know why,

Why do men cheat
Steal and lie,

It seems so funny
When I come home,

Like someone was here
And free to roam,

I see things in places
That I know they shouldn't be,

I tried to confront him
I asked who is she,

What are you talking about
Is what I always get,

It seems like money's missing
Every time that I sit,

I check my records
Bank accounts and phone,

Every night at twelve
I'm sleeping all alone,

To whom it may concern
Can you hear my cry,

My life is flashing away
I'm not ready to die,

Not ready to go
But to keep living a life,

Weather I'm a single mother
Or still his wife...

The Price to Get Ahead

To whom it may concern
I'm writing this to you,

To let you know
What I said was not true,

I lied about it all
I lied from the start,

Every word from my mouth
Was like a shooting dart,

Aiming first
And then I threw,

To get ahead
If only you knew,

It's hard out here
And I can't change,

It's hard for me
To expand my range,

It's been so long
Yet I've stayed strong,

It's been so long
I've never done wrong,

Until today
As I'm writing this to you,

To Whom It May Concern
My job is over with nothing left to do,

And to those that's been waiting
Longing for this day,

Well for you
I have nothing to say...

Poor Customer Service

To Whom It May Concern
I would like to know,

I visited your store
A few days ago,

The service I received
I was not pleased,

I felt I received a lemon
And that I was being teased,

I asked for one thing
But you sold me two,

I asked for a red
But you sold me a blue,

I paid for this
But was sold the other,

I paid for that
And you charged me for another,

To Whom It May Concern
Do you care about your consumer,

Or is your advertisement
"We care for your needs," just a rumor,

Just know my complaint
Will not stop here,

For your company soon
Will have a lot more to fear...

The Trust is Gone

To Whom It May Concern
I really don't understand,

Why is it hard for people
To lend a helping hand,

Can I not be trusted
My word carries no weight,

Did I use all nine lives
I thought I used eight,

Just what did I do
To upset the sphere,

At one point they spoke
But now they stare in fear,

It just seems to me
First this makes no sense,

All I needed was help
But they put up a defense,

Come on now
It shouldn't matter how or what I ask,

I needed help
So I can complete my task,

Just a little help
That's all, not much from them,

To Whom It May Concern
I thought a friendship was a gem,

Something precious
A bond between two,

I just don't understand
What would you do...

What is a Real Man

To Whom It May Concern
I need answer for this,

Does a real man
Always raise his fist,

Tell me please
What is a real man,

Does he help around the house
Does he offer you a hand,

Tell me please
I need to know,

Does he listen to his wife
Or is what he say go,

Tell me please
What does he do,

Does he love you so much
No need to cheat on you,

Tell me I ask
What does he look like,

Does he love to recreate
Associate and ride a bike,

Tell me, O' tell me
Can any be found,

Are there any real men
Still hanging around,

The one that is open
And express how he feels,

Not holding back from me
But showing me what's real,

Supplying that need
Filling that void that I miss,

To Whom It May Concern
All I want is a kiss,

To be held to be loved
That's all I need,

Or is a Real Man
Just a Fairy Tale you read...

The Meat Lovers Special

To Whom It May Concern
I need some advice,

I been a little naughty
Not once and not twice,

See I love my steaks
And my rib bones too,

I love my beef patties
What am I to do,

I walk pass it
It's either thin or thick,

I yearn to taste it
I just want to lick,

First it stands here
Then I see it there,

It drives me crazy
To see beef everywhere,

I crave to touch it
The smell is alluring,

Attractive it is
And still I'm enduring,

But yet temptation
Is getting the best,

To Whom It May Concern
Maybe I just need a rest,

It's too much out here
For me to be satisfied with one,

I need to live life
I need to have fun,

I need to enjoy
All the different types of beef,

Sirloin, Tenderloins,
Certified, Organic, Natural beef,

Yes enjoy everything
All I can eat,

Regret later
For now enjoy meat...

Encouragement for You

To whom it may concern
May your dreams come true,

May all the thing you look for
Be bestowed upon you,

May all the happiness and joy
Be given to you as a gift,

Slow for you to enjoy them
Not so fast, not so swift,

May each day for you
Be greater than the last,

Helping you to forget
All the pain of the past,

May each moment in your life
Be more pleasant than the first,

Providing great energy & strength
That your heart may burst,

That it may be overflowed
With strong love from all around,

And encouragement from true friends
That will never let you down,

To whom it my concern
Please carry this on your heart,

That true love is out there
And it will never depart,

It will never leave you
And it will stay by your side,

So open your heart to it
Yes open it up wide...

Get to the Point

To whom it may concern
I am writing this to you,

Why is the truth not told
About everything you do,

Can not one word that you say
Not travel around in space,

Why not just express yourself
And keep it in one place,

Why the bush must be beaten
Has it done wrong,

Why must I be patient
As your points take so long,

Can we try the direct approach
Without a song and dance,

Can you start over again
I'll give you one more chance,

To whom it my concern
I know you feel my pain,

It's only the truth
That I'm trying to gain,

Life is to short already
With so much for me to do,

So be straight forward with me
Is my advice for you...

Is Life worth Living

To Whom It May Concern
Please hear my pain,

Is it more to life
Than just this to gain,

Every day I wake
I want to give up,

To continue to live
I might just erupt,

It is so easy
Just to give in,

Why do I feel
The need to sin,

Nobody is perfect
Who would want to be,

Living in this life
No one I can see,

Today it's about me
And the life I love,

So many don't care
When they push or shove,

To Whom It May Concern
Please again hear my cry,

I feel the need
The urge to die,

Please help and save
A sorrow lost soul,

Show that there is more to life
Than just striving for gold...

How Confused are We

To Whom It May Concern
I need to express myself,

What is my condition
When it come to my health,

If I travel the world
If I go across land,

I live in a world
Where no one understand,

Confused I might be
But are you too,

If not
Help me find my way through,

Locked in this world
It's hard to get out,

Can you see now
What this is about,

To Whom It May Concern
We are questioned every day,

If you read between the lines
Can you read what I say,

No answer is provided
Directly to your face,

But when you do find it
Will it put you in your place...

Trying to Hold On

To Whom It May Concern
I need to let you know,

Things don't go well
When it's hard to let go,

We been through so much
Many years it has been,

A crack on my heart
For every time they sin,

I want to leave
But it's hard to get out,

Hoping for one day
My true love to sprout,

I know it takes time
And that true person is inside,

If that's the case
Why do I feel the need to hide,

To Whom It May Concern
I love them so much,

I love everything about them
How they feel how they touch,

But it's hard to keep going
With no reason to live,

Especially when you gave
All that you can give…

Living the Double Life

To whom it may concern
I'm grieving today,

I did not know
That I would be left this way,

Lost I am
Confused in light,

How did I let darkness
Cause me to loss sight,

I done so much wrong
It will be hard to forgive,

Once I tell them
About the life I've lived,

I've been living a lie
I've been living in shame,

Sad to say
I'm only to blame,

I could have stopped
I could have quit,

But once you had it
You want another hit,

To whom it may concern
I need strength from you,

To let my other half know
All I put them through,

I am a good person
But yet I am also bad,

Would you keep living a lie
So as not to make them sad,

What would you do
Please let me know,

Confused I am
On which way to go...

Is It Love

To whom it may concern
The timing is not right,

I said no to him again
Late last night,

I really wanted to
But it was hard to give in,

I wouldn't know how
To live with this sin,

The fact of knowing
All I did wrong,

Living in shame
Not knowing for how long,

To whom it may concern
Do you think we are to be,

If he was really in love
Then he would wait like me,

No rushing
Just taking our time,

But I think
He will commit a crime,

He may not hold out
He might just leave,

Maybe we should do it
Later this eve,

We do love each other
I want him to know how much,

I guess the time is right
We can finally touch...

What is Real Trust

To whom it may concern
Can you explain this to me,

What ever happened
To trust and honesty,

Everywhere I turn
And everywhere I look,

I find someone
That just got took,

Took for granted
Raped I would say,

Because their emotions
Got in their way,

Too many are blind
Hard to stay focus,

Until they get bit
By a dishonest locust,

But who is to blame
The one clamming honesty,

Or the one searching
For the right policy,

To whom it may concern
Please help me understand,

Should one just put
All their hopes in one man,

Or woman at that
For they all play a part,

In gaining yet deceiving
An individual heart...

Let You Voice Be Heard

To whom it may concern
Let your voice be heard,

No need to hold back
Express every word,

Tell me how you feel
What's on your mind,

You know hesitation
Keep you left behind,

Take every opportunity
Every moment you have,

To let them know
You are part of this staff,

This unit this relationship
Or whatever it might be,

Don't give up
But make them see,

To whom it may concern
Just speak, speak, and speak,

Don't let them take you
As for someone weak,

Someone unworthy
With nothing to say,

That they can step
Each and every day,

Regardless how hard it is
You have to try,

So stop thinking about it
And wondering why...

The Match-Maker

To whom it may concern
This is short and sweet,

I have someone
I would like for you to meet,

They're nice, caring
Loving and kind,

I told them about you
Hope you don't mind,

The good things you do
Not mentioning the bad,

After hearing about you
They seemed happy and glad,

To whom it may concern
I hope you're not upset,

They have their own
Plus no pets,

Any way
The choice is up to you,

If you want to meet them
Here's their number too,

Do what you want
Do what you may wish,

Just know the sea
Is running out of good fish...

Thank You

To Whom It May Concern
I'm writing this to you,

Thanking all of you
For the things you do,

Reading my work
The poetry I write,

As I stay up every hour
Of every night,

Asking how many times
Did I use this expression,

Am I taking this
In the right direction,

As I say this
I now look up,

Take a deep breath
And a sip from my cup,

So to whom it may concern
I once again thank you all,

Hopefully to my Love
I didn't drop the ball,

In delivering this message
And an Avenue out,

To Whom It May Concern
Was worth writing about......

And What

Happens Now…

And What Happens Now

Put yourself in their shoes and travel along,
All it takes is for one to do wrong,

What start off good can always go bad,
Imagine what kind of relationship they had,

The best of friends through thick-n-thin,
Can you just picture, the places they've been,

The joys they shared, the hard ships they faced,
One before the other is how they were placed,

Smiles for days, no worries no tears,
By each others side with nothing to fear,

But then something happened, no details provided,
Dig deep into the story as you are guided,

Through the ooh, ah and wow,
In the poetic skit *And What Happens Now*......

How can I help ease the pain,

How can I restore life into those veins,

How can I show the sincerity in my words,

How can I show action behind my verbs,

How can I prove my feelings are true,

How can I prove my friendship to you,

How can I show that my concern is real,

How can I express the truth behind how I feel,

How can I, please, I need to know,

How can I help restore that glow,

How can I remove that frown from your face,

How can I put a smile in its place,

How can I, what am I suppose to do,

How can I regain my trust with you...

I know you might be hurt, I hear it in your voice,

But you must remember, you made this choice,

You talked about me to others, did you forget,

Told them about my personal life bit by bit,

I treated you like family, as you came through the door,

I mentioned things to you that only my brother or sister would know,

I poured out my heart, and even cried tears with you,

These are the things that only true friends do,

We talked to each other,

Expressed our feelings with one another,

I told you about my goals and the things I want,

You wanted a nice car, house, with a picket fence in the front,

I shared everything my whole life was in your hand,

But you played the role and back stabbed your friend,

That right there showed me how you feel,

You're fake, phony; your friendship is not real,

And if you really want to know the answer to how,

Just know that your friendship is really foul…

If it is like that, then I can understand,

But I really want to regain my friend,

I know I've done wrong and my ways aren't right,

Look, I don't want to argue and fight,

Let's make ends meet, accept my apology please,

Don't give me the cold shoulder; I don't want to freeze,

I'm sorry, I'm sorry, don't let me drown,

Don't let our friendship run into the ground,

Things could be different if you let me try,

Trust me I don't want our friendship to die,

You never will hear lies from me again,

I still want to be your true best friend,

Forgive me, forgive me, for all the wrong I've done,

Let's go back to having fun…

I know you didn't say start all over again,

Like I told you last time, it's about to end,

I can't trust you anymore, what don't you understand,

You did so much wrong, you are not worthy of a friend,

You disrespected me without me knowing,

I don't think this relationship is growing,

I'm furious, upset, and even hurt,

To me your friendship is not worth dirt,

You betrayed the bond we had,

You killed my joys and made me sad,

I never cried so hard until today,

And all you can think about is going to play,

Please, you better get your mind right,

If you think we are friends, you better think twice,

Better yet, I don't care how long you think,

Your ship has sailed and it's about to sink...

Have I not treated you fair,

Did I not show you that extra love and care,

Have I not been there when times got tough,

Was I not there for you when folks called your bluff,

Was I not there when you got into that fight,

I too was throwing punches left and right,

And I always go hang out with you,

Even when I may be tired too,

But these are things I choose to do,

I did it all just for you,

I can continue on about the past,

But we know how long this debate will last,

So I will continue to discuss what is taking place here,

Although it may be the end I fear,

Whatever it takes I'm willing to do,

To restore the relationship between me and you...

What can you do you ask,

You are not worthy of any task,

You did so much, but little is what you see,

The numerous times that you have hurt me,

The important things you tend to forget,

Is what tossed this relationship into the pit,

The hurt I experienced by what you did,

Made me feel like a little kid,

I felt like a pawn in your hand,

You just abused me as your friend,

But now you want to mention all you've done for me,

When were you there? Name any time so I'll believe,

As I recall it, you weren't there for my fight,

You said you had more important things to do that night,

Saying you made those tired trips for me,

If you were so tired, you should've just let me be,

I never forced you into anything, the choice was yours,

Being fake, phony and lying, is what's closing the doors,

To our friendship, it has ended, I'm over, and we're done,

Now you can go run off and have your fun...

Person 1

I understand you now,

But just tell me how,

How and what I did to you,

How am I losing your friendship too,

As these tears pour from my eyes,

All I want to know is why,

Why is this coming to an end,

Why don't you want to be my friend,

What did I do, oh, what did I do,

Do you think I intended to hurt you,

Tell me what I did wrong please, please, please,

The pain is what I'm trying to ease,

Was it something I did, or something I said,

If it's that bad, then you've been mislead,

I admit that I've done wrong and that is true,

But explain to me the facts on how I hurt you…

The facts are simple I'm surprised you don't see,

The wrong in what you did to me,

First it's not something you did,

But it's the secrets you hid,

Lies about you doing this and that,

When we both know the real fact,

You weren't there for me when I needed you most,

All you ever did was brag and boast,

About yourself and the things you had,

Knowing that you were trying to make me mad,

Then when I tried to talk to you,

All you made reference to was you know who,

Then talked about my life and the way I live,

I gave this friendship all that I could give,

You did so much the list can go on for days,

You will never change your ugly, fake, foul ways,

You'll never grow up; you act like a child,

The way you view life is stupid and wild,

There's no meaning to life behind you at all,

You try to bring others down to make yourself look tall,

But I'm going to be quiet now this is the life you chose,

This argument is senseless and coming to a close...

You know, I know what this is all about,

So why don't we just let it all come out,

You're jealous, aren't you, jealous of me,

That's the only reason that I can see,

When it comes to the accomplishments I've made, and the things I own,

You want to be just like me, you even want my home,

You don't accept your mistakes; they're not your fault,

You talk about me hiding secrets, fool you the one that got caught,

Trying to throw all your problems my way,

Hush your mouth, there's nothing more you can say,

But I think you're right, this needs to end,

Because I can't stand to have a jealous friend,

You say I'm fake, phony, and foul,

I'm going to let you think on that for a while,

Better yet I don't care what you say or think,

Your jealous friendship is starting to reek,

Let me get away, you're right I don't need you anymore,

What do I need a jealous and stinky friend like you for...

Me jealous of you, you got your nerve,

This is exactly why I'm kicking you to the curb,

You just don't understand, you'll never get it right,

I don't see how you even sleep at night,

After all we've been through, after all we had,

I rather see you more happy then sad,

I rather see you smile from ear to ear,

But you always acted like you couldn't hear,

I broke bread with you and shared my pain,

A friendship with you I strived to maintain,

Day in and day out I was always hurt,

I was the one being treated like dirt,

You hurt me so bad and embarrassed me too,

How would you feel if you were in my shoes,

And now you claim that I'm the bogus one here,

You're the one crying all these tears,

Me jealous of you, you better get real,

You're living off of me we know the real deal,

That's why it's over, over I said,

This relationship is over, done, and dead...

Wow, since you put it like that,

Maybe I really was a rat,

Maybe everything about me wasn't right,

I know I never paid attention to the light,

I was stubborn and I was a fool,

Nothing I did was ever cool,

I know I was a pain in the neck,

But I never wanted this to end in a wreck,

I was stupid and acted like a kid,

I didn't care about the things you ever did,

I hurt you, which was not my intention to do,

I know I never really meant to hurt you,

Our friendship means a lot to me,

You opened me up in ways I couldn't see,

 I tried to give you my best, and my all,

But now I understand your judgment call,

So if it's over, it's over, said and done,

Let's go our separate ways before the setting of the sun...

Hold on let me think things through,

Maybe it's really not worth losing you,

We've been through so much for so long,

Can you recall our favorite song,

I know we had our ups and our downs,

But that's no reason to kick this friendship out of town,

Let's try to maintain the relationship we once had,

And try not to get each other mad,

We make mistakes in life; we all have our flaws,

I guess that's no reason to put this friendship on pause,

So my response to all that was said today,

I would love for things to be the old way,

Go back to the relationship that once was here,

No more pain, no more crying a tear,

Just two best friends enjoying the good times,

Like apples and oranges, and lemons and limes,

Starting all over is not a bad idea at all,

I guess this is my final judgment call,

The decision is now in your hands,

Do you still want to remain best friends...

www.ingramcontent.com/pod-product-compliance
Lightning Source LLC
Chambersburg PA
CBHW031525040426
42445CB00009B/406

* 9 7 8 0 5 7 8 0 8 2 3 4 9 *